GOOD AND ANGRY

Your Personal Guide To Anger Management

By John Marshall

Copyright © 2003 by John Marshall

Good And Angry,Your Personal Guide To Anger Management
by by John Marshall

Printed in the United States of America
ISBN 0974069302

All rights reserved. This book or parts thereof may not be reproduced in any form, stored in a retrieval system, or transmitted in any form by any means—electronic, mechanical, photocopy, recording, or otherwise—without prior written permission of the publisher, except as provided by United States copyright law.

Unless otherwise quoted, all Scripture quotations are from the New American Standard Version of the Bible. Copyright © 1960, 1962, 1963, 1968, 1971, 1972, 1973, 1975, 1977, 1995 by the Lockman Foundation, a Corporation Not for Profit

Scripture quotations marked KJV are from the King James Version of the Bible.

Scripture quotations marked NKJV are from the Holy Bible, New King James Version. Copyright © 1982 Thomas Nelson, Inc.

Scripture quotations marked NIV are from the Holy Bible, New International Version. Copyright © 1973, 1978, 1984, International Bible Society.

Scripture quotations marked NLT are from the Holy Bible, New Living Translation. Copyright © 1996 by Tyndale House Publishers, Inc., Wheaton, IL 60189.

Editor: Tom Gill

Dedication

I dedicate this book to my mother, Mrs. Annie Sue Boyd Marshall, (1915-). For all of my life she has displayed a superior stamina as she exercised her spiritual strength. Indeed, she is my heroine.

In 1958, my baby sister became ill. The doctors prescribed the wrong medication and it permanently damaged her brain, thereby retarding her mental development. Mother has always been her primary caretaker. For forty-five (45) years mother has had to plan her every day around the needs of my sister. As unfortunate and demanding as this hasbeen, mother has never expressed bitterness, hatefulness or resentment. For many this would have been a burden; but for mother this has become a blessing.

Throughout all her adversities in life, she has remained both good and angry. Never, not once, do I recall her allowing anger to cause her to respond inappropriately. May God forever smile favorably upon her is my prayer.

Mother: You are the greatest! There is none like you in all the earth.

TABLE OF CONTENTS

Introduction 9
Chapter 1   The Decision Is Mine. 11
Chapter 2   Be Responsible With Anger . 27
Chapter 3   The Problem With Anger
            Is Me. 41
Chapter 4   Violence—Anger's Deadly
            Ground 63
Chapter 5   Godly Anger Gets Results . . 87
About the Author. 105

INTRODUCTION

Do you struggle with anger?

Do you find yourself in situations where anger begins to boil inside of you till it finally erupts like a volcano?

Is it possible to be both good and angry at the same time?

Are you ready to learn what anger is all about and how to use this powerful emotion to glorify God?

Anger is one of the least understood and most over abused emotions God has given us. On one hand, we're told not to be angry or that it's bad to be angry. While on the other, we're told to express our anger and not to stifle it. What's the truth?

This book will help you learn about godly anger and how God has invested you with the ability to utilize anger to bring about His purpose on earth. Anger is a God-given emotion, but you must learn how to use it and become effective in its expression in order to be fully matured in Christ.

Jesus became angry. God has shown His anger. Moses was angry as were other men written about in the Scriptures. So anger isn't a foreign emotion that should be deported to another land. Take hold of the promises of God and the power of the Holy Spirit as you read this book, and you'll learn when, why, and how anger should be expressed.

Chapter One
1 The Decision Is Mine

*Be angry, and yet do not sin;
do not let the sun go down
on your anger...*

(Eph. 4:26)

The Decision Is Mine

"I'll show them. Then they'll be sorry for what they've done. I'll get the last word this time."

With a pounding heart and vowing to get even, Kenny stormed out of the room. He'd finally been pushed too far—or so he thought.

Do you have a "button" that gets pushed every now and then throwing you into an almost uncontrollable rage? Do you realize that your anger is the result of decisions you've made?

You Must Deliberately Decide To Be Angry

Think back to a time when you were most angry, angrier than you had ever been before. Do you remember just how angry you were? Could you measure your anger? If so, was it measured by an increase in your heart rate or by the cost of the dishes you had to replace?

Are you still as angry today as you were then? If not, what happened to your anger? How would you be affected if all your angers were compounded together?

You can see by all these questions, and many more that could be asked, that anger is a very complex emotion. Anger is so complex, that it almost defies a logical, rational explanation. Especially if you're the one who is angry!

Psychologists have said much about anger. However, through the Scriptures, God has more accurately informed us about anger. Therefore, to please God, we must approach our anger with a biblical perspective.

The people of God must deliberately decide to be angry. Yes, you ought to be angry sometimes to fulfill your citizenship requirements. Nevertheless, anger must be a deliberate choice.

The apostle Paul wrote: "Be angry, and

yet do not sin; do not let the sun go down on your anger" (Eph. 4:26). This exhortation suggests control over your emotions, and the ability to be angry with no sin. Therefore, becoming angry must be a deliberate decision, like a tool used with skill.

Anger Defined

Anger is a settled and abiding habit of the mind that is aroused under certain conditions. When you become angry, you have decided, based upon certain conditions, to elevate your emotional intensity to the level of anger. The biblical story of the prodigal son in Luke 15 serves as a good illustration.

The younger of two sons went to his father and demanded his inheritance. When he received it, he quickly squandered it away on parties and wild living. Finally, broke, dejected and eating with the hogs, he decided to return to his father's house.

Meanwhile, the father longed to see his son, so he stood by the gate watching for him to return. At last, in the distance he saw him coming. Immediately, the father set in motion a party to celebrate the return on his wayward son. A fatted calf was prepared, a new coat and ring were put on the young man, and the party went into full swing.

The older brother was working in the fields when his brother came home, so he wasn't aware of what the big celebration was about. When he inquired of his father and was told that his brother had come home, he became angry. No matter how the father pleaded, the older son's anger remained.

The older brother reacted to the events surrounding his younger brother's return and responded with anger. Though a reaction at first, it became a deliberate response—a decision to be angry.

Scripture Demands Anger

Ephesians 4:6 declares, "Be angry, and yet do not sin...." The demand of anger suggests that we should be angry. The word "be" is a present imperative; it commands action.

The apostle Paul, writing for God, commands anger. Notice he doesn't say, "if" you are angry, but "be" angry. When God says to "be" anything, we are compelled to comply. Therefore, we can see that anger must be a deliberate decision.

God decided to respond with anger:

And you shall not wrong a stranger or oppress him, for you were strangers in

the land of Egypt. You shall not afflict any widow or orphan. If you afflict him at all, and if he does cry out to Me, I will surely hear his cry; and My anger will be kindled, and I will kill you with the sword; and your wives shall become widows and your children fatherless.
                    (Exodus 22:21-24)

This Scripture clearly shows a warning of God's anger being kindled if His people were abused or afflicted by another. God declared His decision to be angry and subsequently warned the people about it.

We can further see the weight of God's anger when He declared, "My anger will be kindled..." The King James Version renders it "My wrath will wax hot." God declares that if anyone was guilty of afflicting His people, He had decided beforehand to be angry. This again illustrates the deliberate nature of God's anger, which we are to emulate.

Our anger should stem from a deliberate decision, not a rash reaction. If we are ever angry, it must be because we have weighed the situation and decided that anger is the proper response. We must never become angry "accidentally." It must be a deliberate decision.

There are times when anger is the proper

response, and times when it isn't. Times when you should be angry and times when you shouldn't. If God wants you to be angry and you're not, then you do Him a disservice—you're walking in disobedience and stand in danger of God becoming angry with you. Likewise, if you are angry when you shouldn't be, you fall into sin and do God a disservice.

Therefore, in order to please God, be angry when He requires it. Don't become angry by default; become angry by design.

Five Biblical Reasons To Choose Anger

Becoming angry by design means that you listen to the Holy Spirit and obey His voice. To help you understand, let's consider several different reasons for anger.

Choice #1: Anger towards those who oppress the weak.

> Thus has the LORD of hosts said, 'Dispense true justice, and practice kindness and compassion each to his brother; and do not oppress the widow or the orphan, the stranger or the poor; and do not devise evil in your hearts against one another.'
>
> (Zech. 7:9-10)

When the defenseless are oppressed, we are to be angry. Notice how God mentions widows and orphans. He does so because they are especially defenseless. Therefore, God has repeatedly warned us not to oppress them.

God delivered those who were oppressed:

> Moses was educated in all the learning of the Egyptians, and he was a man of power in words and deeds. But when he was approaching the age of forty, it entered his mind to visit his brethren, the sons of Israel. And when he saw one of them being treated unjustly, he defended him and took vengeance for the oppressed by striking down the Egyptian. And he supposed that his brethren understood that God was granting them deliverance through him; but they did not understand.
> (Acts 7:22-25)

Choice #2: Anger toward those who sow discouragement.

Then Caleb quieted the people before Moses, and said, "We should by all means go up and take possession of

it, for we shall surely overcome it." But the men who had gone up with him said, "We are not able to go up against the people, for they are too strong for us." So they gave out to the sons of Israel a bad report of the land which they had spied out, saying, "The land through which we have gone, in spying it out, is a land that devours its inhabitants; and all the people whom we saw in it are men of great size. There also we saw the Nephilim (the sons of Anak are part of the Nephilim); and we became like grasshoppers in our own sight, and so we were in their sight."
(Num. 13:30-33)

God gave the land of Canaan to the children of Israel through His covenant with Abraham. The Promised Land was "flowing with milk and honey," a beautiful, fertile land of plenty.

When the Israelites neared the border of the land, Moses sent twelve spies to gather information and bring back a report. Two of the twelve brought an encouraging report, while the other ten lamented the strength of the inhabitants. Their negative report created such despondency in the people that they decided not to enter the very land that

God had given them.

Sadly, because the people received the report of the ten and rejected the report of the two, God's anger was kindled against them. Instead of inheriting the land, an entire generation had to die. These folk were barred from the land of their inheritance because of the unbelief in their hearts (Numbers 32:1-15; Acts 13:1-13).

Choice #3: Anger toward detractors of Jesus.

Jesus came to show us the Father, and to demonstrate what God was and is like. Jesus was and is the expressed image of His Father (Col. 1:15), and He perfectly modeled His life after the Father.

When detractors attempt to discredit Jesus or detour us from our theological responsibilities, godly anger should well up within us. We can see throughout Scripture how God has assigned responsibilities to His people. Just as a supervisor writes a memo to his or her employees to assign responsibilities, so God has written us a memo—the Bible. It is His memo to us through which He assigns responsibilities.

People will always oppose the Lord and be detractors of Him. They will seek to confuse your understanding of what God has said and will seek to lead you into disobedience, much like children trying to get another child into trouble.

Like Jesus, you should be angry when detractors seek to interfere with your God-given responsibilities. Jesus Christ became angry when His detractors interfered with His theological responsibility. Jesus came into the world to demonstrate total conformity to the authoritative Word of God, and He allowed no person to thwart His purpose.

The Pharisees, Sadducees and scribes had developed many traditions. Often their traditions conflicted with the word of God. Jesus said to them, "But in vain do they worship Me, teaching as doctrines the precepts of men. Neglecting the commandment of God in order to keep our tradition" (Mark 7:7-8). Again, He would say, "… And by this you invalidated the word of God for the sake of your tradition" (Matthew 15:6).

Jesus perceived the opposition of the Pharisees, "after looking around at them with anger, grieved at their hardness of heart" (Mark 3:5). Their calloused hearts had become so hardened that they were beyond sensitivity and feeling, even the words of Jesus could not penetrate them.

Calloused people, such as the Pharisees described above, disturb the faith of others. Therefore, when we see people with such hardened hearts, we ought to become angry.

Choice #4: *Anger toward those who oppose.*

Jesus became angry with those who intensely opposed Him because they interfered with His purpose. "He entered again into a synagogue; and a man was there with a withered hand. And they were watching Him to see if He would heal him on the Sabbath, in order that they might accuse Him" (Mark 3:1-2).

Notice that this crowd was waiting to accuse Jesus. They weren't interested in seeing the mighty hand of God move, nor did they care about the man whose hand was withered. They only sought to discredit Jesus.

This type of opposition is purposeful in its aim to discredit the works of God. This purposeful opposition angered Jesus, as it should anger you. When you face a detractor that opposes Jesus, become angry. Let the passion rise in you and take charge of the situation at hand.

"He [Jesus] said to the man with the withered hand, 'Rise and *come* forward!' And He said to them, 'Is it lawful on the Sabbath to do good or to do harm, to save a life or to kill?'" (Mark 3:3-4). Those opposing Jesus argued about the allowances of the Law, but Jesus told them they misunderstood the Law. The traditions they had developed violated God's original intent for the Law, so Jesus asked if it was lawful to save a life or kill. Scripture says the Pharisees remained silent.

Those opposed to Jesus were not only purposeful in their opposition, but they were persistent as well. They remained silent because they knew that any answer would condemn them. This is akin to a jury that observes the innocence of the accused, but refuses to vote "not guilty."

Jesus asked the question, but the Pharisees refused to answer. They persisted in their opposition, which interfered with Jesus' theological responsibility. Therefore, Jesus became angry. So should you.

Choice #5: Anger toward disciples who interfere with social responsibilities.
Immediately following a text on divorce, the gospel writer, Mark, wrote about children. Often, children of divorce are permanently scarred. We must ask, were the subjects of divorce and children deliberately written about together? Were these subjects placed together for a theological purpose?

And they were bringing children to Him so that He might touch them; and the disciples rebuked them. But when Jesus saw this, He was indignant and said to them, "Permit the children to come to Me; do not hinder them; for the kingdom of God belongs to such as these. Truly I say to you, whoever does not receive the kingdom of God like a child shall not enter it at all." And He took them in His arms and began blessing them, laying His hands upon them.

(Mark 10:13-16)

Jesus welcomed the children. Undoubtedly, Jesus felt a social responsibility to welcome the children, even though His disciples tried to shoo them away. We can see how Jesus rebuked the disciples for interfering with His interaction with the little ones. In fact, Jesus became indignant!

Children were then, and still are a vital contributing arm of society. Little ones are necessary, not only to this generation, but for those to come as well. Therefore, when insensitive adults rebuke children for being social, it's a time to become angry.

Likewise, when other disciples interfere with our interaction with children, we must respond with anger. We have a responsibility to the children. Therefore, when our responsibilities toward them are unfulfilled, we ought to become angry.

Right Decision—Right Timing

The key is understanding that anger is a decision. Because it's a decision, you must consider the need to make the right decision at the right time. Anger out of control is destructive and can be deadly, but anger rightly placed and rightly timed is like a surgeon's scalpel revealing tissue that must be excised.

We'll discuss this more in the next chapter, but before we go on, pray this prayer:

> *Heavenly Father. Thank You for giving me all my emotions, including anger. Help me to hear Your voice so I can know when to be angry and how angry to be. Help me to be angry without sin so that I can maintain my witness of godly character for all to see. In Jesus' Name, Amen.*

Chapter Two

BE RESPONSIBLE WITH ANGER

*Be angry, and yet do not sin;
do not let the sun go down
on your anger, and do not give
the devil an opportunity.*

(Ephesians 4:26-27)

BE RESPONSIBLE WITH ANGER

"I can't believe I flew off the handle like that." thought Joan. "I'm not an angry person. Is there something wrong with me?"

"Joan." Minister Williams said. "Everyone has to learn how to handle their anger. One way is by understanding how to respond properly in situations that challenge you. Let's look at some Scriptures that will help shed light on what I mean..."

To Become Angry Is Your Choice

Becoming angry is a choice you make. However, the choice of anger can sometimes be detrimental to the situation at hand. Much depends upon why you are angry and how it fits God's plan. Answer these questions:

- Do you become angry most often by design or default?
- Are you ever deliberately angry when you should be deliberately not angry?

Let's look at some reasons not to be angry.

Reason #1: Rejection is no cause for anger.

> Now the man had relations with his wife Eve, and she conceived and gave birth to Cain, and she said, "I have gotten a manchild with the help of the LORD." And again, she gave birth to his brother Abel. And Abel was a keeper of flocks, but Cain was a tiller of the ground. So it came about in the course of time that Cain brought an offering to the LORD of the fruit of the ground.

And Abel, on his part also brought of the firstlings of his flock and of their fat portions. And the LORD had regard for Abel and for his offering; but for Cain and for his offering He had no regard. So Cain became very angry and his countenance fell.

Then the LORD said to Cain, "Why are you angry? And why has your countenance fallen? If you do well, will not your countenance be lifted up? And if you do not do well, sin is crouching at the door; and its desire is for you, but you must master it."

And Cain told Abel his brother. And it came about when they were in the field, that Cain rose up against Abel his brother and killed him.

(Gen 4:1-8)

Cain did not do well. Notice that God warned him of the sin that crouched at his door, but Cain didn't acknowledge it. Furthermore, because of his rejection of God, God rejected him. Cain chose anger instead of repentance, wrath instead of submission, and was cursed because of it.

Reason #2: Jealousy is no cause for anger.

"Now the word of the LORD came to Jonah the second time, saying, 'Arise, go to Nineveh the great city and proclaim to it the proclamation which I am going to tell you'"

(Jonah 3:1-2).

Nineveh was a very great, but a very proud city. The residents, from the king to the lowliest slave had turned from God and were serving idols. Nevertheless, God loved them.

Jonah was sent by God to this great city to proclaim the Day of the Lord's wrath if they didn't repent and turn from their wicked ways. Jonah's warning from God was received by the entire city, so God lifted His hand of judgment and spared their lives. "So Jonah began to go through the city one day's walk; and he cried out and said, 'Yet forty days and Nineveh will be overthrown.' Then the people of Nineveh believed in God; and they called a fast and put on sackcloth from the greatest to the least of them. When the word reached the king of Nineveh, he arose from his throne, laid aside his robe from him, covered himself with sackcloth and sat on the ashes. He issued a proclamation and it said, 'In Nineveh by the decree of the king and his nobles: Do not let man, beast, herd, or flock taste a thing. Do not let them eat or drink water. 'But both man and beast must be covered with sackcloth; and let men call on God earnestly that each man turn from his wicked way and from the violence which is in his hands. Who knows, God may turn and relent and withdraw His burning anger so that we will not perish." When God saw their deeds, that they turned from their wicked way, then God relented concerning the calamity which He had declared He would bring upon the, And he did not do it." (Jonah 3:3-10).

Rather than glory in the Lord that Nineveh was saved, Jonah instead became angry and bitter. "But it greatly displeased Jonah, and he became angry" (Jonah 4:1). God's grace and mercy showered on Nineveh revealed a dark place in Jonah's heart that needed the light of God to be exposed.

Therefore, God asked Jonah a very compelling question: "…should I not have compassion on Nineveh, the great city in which there are more than 120,000 persons who do not know *the difference* between their right and left hand, as well as many animals?" (Jonah 4:11) Through that exchange, God showed Jonah that he had no right to be angry.

Your Proper Response In Anger

Just as you deliberately decide to be angry, you must deliberately decide not to be angry. Do you get angry at work and bring it home to your family? Or, do you get angry at home and carry it to work or school and make others pay? Do you get angry with your spouse or children and then take it out on the folks at church?

How should you respond when you're angry?

Proper Response #1: Let God exact vengeance and retribution.

Your response in anger must not include vengeance. Retaliation, revenge, retribution, and getting even are all part of vengeance. Vengeance is "do unto others because they have done unto you," which is contrary to the Word of God.

Retaliation is never appropriate. The Lord declares that vengeance belongs to Him, and that He will judge His people. Therefore, when you try to even the score, even if you are legitimately angry, you usurp the role God has reserved for Himself alone. The apostle Paul wrote:

Never pay back evil for evil to anyone. Respect what is right in the sight of all men. If possible, so far as it depends on you, be at peace with all men. Never take your own revenge, beloved, but leave room for the wrath of God, for it is written,

> *"VENGEANCE IS MINE, I WILL REPAY," says the Lord.*
> *(Rom. 12:17-19)*

God's challenge is for you to respond exactly opposite of vengeance. Therefore, you must ensure that if you're not at peace it's not because of anything that you've done. Paul further wrote:

> *"But if your enemy is hungry, feed him, and if he is thirsty, give him a drink; for in so doing you will heap burning coals upon his head." Do not be overcome by evil, but overcome evil with good.*
> *(Rom. 12:20-21)*

God does not enlist an army of vigilantes to carry out His judgment. Instead, God works within the confines of human law and jurisprudence to execute His retribution. Governments are authorized by God to punish evildoers: "Let every person be in subjection to the governing authorities. For there is no authority except from God, and those which exist are established by God...For rulers are not a cause of fear for good behavior, but for evil" (Rom. 13:1,3).

Proper Response #2: Imitate the life of Christ.

Some behaviors are off-limits; they are unjustified even though you are angry. Response-ability justifies behavior, not anger.

You must respond in a way that is inclusive, though you can ignore those who behave with no integrity. If you want to remain in control while angry, imitate the life of Christ.

> *And He entered again into a synagogue; and a man was there with a withered hand.*
>
> *And they were watching Him to see if He would heal him on the Sabbath, in order that they might accuse Him.*
>
> *And He said to the man with the withered hand, "Rise and come forward!"*
>
> *And He said to them, "Is it lawful on the Sabbath to do good or to do harm, to save a life or to kill?" But they kept silent.*
>
> (Mark 3:1-4)

Did you notice that not everyone present in this crowd was on Jesus' side? Some were there who only wanted to accuse Him. Knowing their hearts, Jesus asked a question that forced them to reanalyze their thoughts. Sadly, the question didn't change their hearts, but hardened them even more. These men had already made up their minds what they would do regardless of what happened. They were without integrity.

When you interact with people who have no integrity, no matter what you say, they'll not be fair. Therefore, be just like Jesus. Ignore their interference and press on with what you know must be done. "And after looking around at them with anger, grieved at their hardness of heart, He said to the man, 'Stretch out your hand.' And he stretched it out, and his hand was restored" (Mark 3:5).

When it was obvious that these folk had no integrity, Jesus didn't say anything else to try and convince them or change their minds. Instead, He commanded the man to stretch out his hand and then healed it. Jesus went on with His business, doing what was the right thing to do.

Don't spend your time arguing with someone who has no integrity. It's not going to make any difference. When you enter into an argument with folk like this, you only become frustrated. Their minds and hearts aren't changed. Furthermore, you increase the risk of behaving in an ungodly manner yourself. Don't go there!

When you've expressed your point, why continue to argue? Jesus ignored the interference of those with no integrity, and so should you. Once you've given your statement of evidence and have no more to submit, and you know the person has understood you, don't repeat it. Jesus only repeated Himself twice, once in Luke 10:41 and the other in Luke 13:3-5. Arguments go nowhere; they only lead to dead ends.

Proper Response #3: Inform those who need to be informed.
Some folk who block you simply need to be informed. They are just ignorant, so inform them.

We see this principle in action when the disciples rebuked children who were gathering around Jesus. These men were not mean ogres who despised children; they thought they were protecting the Lord from any "distractions" causes by little children. However, Jesus made it abundantly clear that they were wrong in their actions.

> *But when Jesus saw this, He was indignant and said to them, "Permit the children to come to Me; do not hinder them; for the kingdom of God belongs to such as these. Truly I say to you, whoever does not receive the kingdom of God like a child shall not enter it at all."*
> (Mark 10:14-15)

There is a difference between those who lack information and those who lack integrity. Therefore, your response to each should be different as well. Ignore those without integrity, but inform those who lack information.

When those who need information are informed, their behavior will change. However, those with no integrity will continue on their destructive path and will even search out others who will assist them.

Jesus ignored the Pharisees and healed a man. They sought out the Herodians, enemies normally, and invited them to join in their plots and plans against Jesus. The Pharisees expressed the attitude: "We don't care whether we've been getting along or not, so long as you're in our group now." Never gang bang like that.

However, when Jesus informed the disciples, they allowed the children to come to Jesus so He could bless them. "And He took them in His arms and *began* blessing them, laying His hands upon them" (Mark 10:16).

People of integrity who simply don't have enough information will behave appropriately when given the information necessary. People with no integrity will continue to behave inappropriately even after the needed information is given.

Be careful to avoid categorizing behavior that grows from a lack of information as that of no integrity. When you believe that someone is behaving out of a lack of integrity, your anger is likely to intensify more than if you know they are just behaving inappropriately out of ignorance.

Anger Is A Decision

Remember, you decide when to be angry and how angry to be, so don't be hasty and don't be nasty. Your anger should rest on a deep cushion of love and respect, with the hope of restoration firmly in place. This demonstrates your integrity in action and presents a godly example for others to witness.

We are the problem when anger gets out of control. During the next chapter we'll discuss problems with anger, including our selves.

Pray this prayer:

Heavenly Father. Grant me the wisdom to behave in an appropriate manner, even when I'm angry. Lord. I only want to lose control to the control of Your Holy Spirit. In Jesus' Name. Amen.

CHAPTER THREE
THE PROBLEM WITH ANGER IS ME

This you know, my beloved brethren. But let everyone be quick to hear, slow to speak and slow to anger; for the anger of man does not achieve the righteousness of God.

(James 1:19-20)

The Problem With Anger Is Me

"I wonder how long they planned that!" thought Bill. Surely his co-workers had conspired against him to make him look foolish.

"Bill. Nobody got together and planned to make you look bad. We were just havin' some fun and it got out of hand." said Steve. "I'm sorry if I've hurt you, and I'll bet the other guys are too."

"Maybe you're right, Steve. I guess I just felt like you all kind of ganged up on me. You know what I mean?"

Bill is dealing with some feelings that are not uncommon among people. Consider these questions: Have you...

- wondered why people seem to hurt you on purpose?
- been accused of doing something you didn't do?
- been told you have an attitude while you thought things were just fine?

Nobody escapes the scrutiny of others. Likewise, people fall under our scrutiny as well. Is this God's way?

Beware of Motive Misinterpretation

If your attitude can be misrepresented, then you can make the same mistake with others. When you automatically think you've been mistreated on purpose, you've jumped right into the seat of the magistrate and judged motives. You haven't given the accused an opportunity to defend herself or clear the air, you've judged her integrity. Why?

This type of judging leads you into ungodly anger. Instead of being angry for a purpose, you become angry for a cause—yours. First, talk to the person. Find out what's going on before you become angry, then you'll know the proper response to the situation and will not react out of immature anger.

When you are angry, you are more apt to respond in an intense manner. This makes the admonition of James very important: "... let everyone be quick to hear, slow to speak *and* slow to anger" (James 1:19).

When you are angry, don't blurt out too quickly what you want to say. Be slow to speak! This admonition, if followed, will allow you to soften your tone and will keep doors open to resolve issues.

You can say just about anything to a person if you do it right. In fact, you can call a man a dog and get away with it if you're careful. You could say, "I hear you're the big dog down there." and the man will just smile. Why? Because you said it right, he took it as a compliment.

Decide How To Respond

Consider your tone. Your anger doesn't justify a harsh tone. The Bible says to, "season your speech with salt" (Colossians 4:6). Know how to respond, not only in tone but in content as well. As important as your tone is the content of your response. Anger doesn't justify cutting, sarcastic or mean responses.

This points out the importance of deciding to be angry and then deciding you response. Just as you must decide in advance those things over which to be angry, decide in advance how you're going to behave.

For example, if I'm driving down the interstate and happen to exceed the speed limit and am pulled over by a patrolman, I've already decided how I'm going to respond. I'm going to hand over whatever he asks for and keep my mouth closed. It doesn't matter how late I am, how fervently I may feel the stop is unwarranted, or whether I think he's picking on me, I have decided how to respond! I'm not going to argue, I'm not going to jump out of the car and go for his gun, I'm not going to go for my gun, and I'm not going to run; I'm going to comply.

This lesson is important for children as well. You need to decide now, that regardless of how angry your parents are or how angry you are, you will still speak to them respectfully. Decide today not to yell at your mother and father; decide today not to argue with them or be disrespectful.

When you get on the school bus, decide not to argue and disagree with the bus driver. The driver is an adult and worthy of respect by virtue of that fact alone, plus he is accountable to others for your welfare. When you get to school and interact with the teachers, aids, office workers and the principle, decide to treat them with respect and dignity. I assure you, that as you do to them, so they will do to you. Decide in advance to say, "Yes, Sir" or "Yes, Ma'am."

The Disciplined Response

Deciding in advance means that you've disciplined yourself to respond in a particular way. Just like a paramedic practices and trains for emergencies, so you should practice and train to respond instead of react.

While hanging on the cross, Jesus said, "Father forgive them, for they know not what they do." Jesus could do that because He had decided in advance how to respond. He knew He was facing the cross and knew what that meant. Though He could have called down ten thousand angels to spare His life, Jesus chose not to get even. He made a decision.

Being a Christian is about making decisions and then having the internal discipline to conform to the decision that's been made. When it comes to anger, your response must come out of a decision you've made, not the heat of the moment. You decide that if you're angry, you'll respond a particular way. Then, when faced with the moment of anger, just like the paramedic, you know how to respond because you've trained for it.

This means that your response will bring healing not more wounds, and reconciliation not division. You've decided to respond in such a way that fellowship will not be injured and rehabilitation can occur.

This is where knowledge of the Word of God is important; it is there that you'll learn the type of responses that are healthy. You may think a human response is appropriate, but the Word of God will guide you to another response that is healthier. As you discover how God works, then your decision is whether or not to obey God. Decide to obey Him. Then, even when you're angry, your response will be appropriate.

The Problem With Anger

Repeat this phrase out loud: *"The Biggest problem with anger is me!"* Once you get a handle on this important truth, you'll be a long way down the road to the proper use and expression of anger.

When we get angry, we tend to stop thinking appropriately. This is the primary reason not to argue with people who are angry. It's a waste of time because they're not thinking appropriately. When a person is angry, they often don't even hear what is being said to them. Their minds have become so focused on the anger that all else slips by unheeded.

You've probably experienced this before. During the course of a heated argument, you can completely switch sides and begin to argue the exact opposite of what you had been arguing. The person with whom you're arguing will do the same so that you both are on the completely opposite side of where you started. This happens because you've stopped reasoning; it has become clouded and of little value.

Often, people will expect you to say one thing even though you have said something else. When that happens, instead of acting on what you've said, they'll react to what they expect you to say. This happens because they're angry and their mind has stopped thinking objectively. Their ability to reason has been impaired causing them to become defensive in their attitude toward you and what you're saying. They're in neutral or even reverse in some situations.

However, God wants you to work through

your anger. You've got to know why you're angry and the purpose it will serve. Only then will you know how to respond according to God's plan and design.

Two Principles of Anger Management

I want to share two principles of anger management with you, and I'll use some experiences of Moses to do so. Scripture declares:

> *Then the sons of Israel, the whole congregation, came to the wilderness of Zin in the first month; and the people stayed at Kadesh. Now Miriam died there and was buried there.*
>
> *And there was no water for the congregation; and they assembled themselves against Moses and Aaron. The people thus contended with Moses and spoke, saying, "If only we had perished when our brothers perished before the LORD! Why then have you brought the LORD 's assembly into this wilderness, for us and our beasts to die here? And why have you made us come up from Egypt, to bring us in to this wretched place? It is not a place of grain or figs*

or vines or pomegranates, nor is there water to drink." Then Moses and Aaron came in from the presence of the assembly to the doorway of the tent of meeting, and fell on their faces. Then the glory of the LORD appeared to them; and the LORD spoke to Moses, saying,

"Take the rod; and you and your brother Aaron assemble the congregation and speak to the rock before their eyes, that it may yield its water. You shall thus bring forth water for them out of the rock and let the congregation and their beasts drink." So Moses took the rod from before the LORD, just as He had commanded him; and Moses and Aaron gathered the assembly before the rock. And he said to them, "Listen now, you rebels; shall we bring forth water for you out of this rock?" Then Moses lifted up his hand and struck the rock twice with his rod; and water came forth abundantly, and the congregation and their beasts drank. But the LORD said to Moses and Aaron, "Because you have not believed Me, to treat Me as holy in the sight of the sons of Israel, therefore you shall not bring this assembly into the land which I have given them."

(Num. 20:1-12)

Principle #1: Acknowledge the problem of your anger.

When you are angry, you must work through your anger. You must acknowledge the problem of your anger, because it can be a very difficult problem. You need to reason within your own heart about your own anger.

It is very important to confront yourself about your anger—you must monitor your anger and police it accordingly. As you do, you'll find yourself responding in an appropriate manner.

Admitting you have a problem with anger and don't handle it properly is the first and most important step to bringing it under control and into God's design. For example, if you know you're angry now and have been angry for the last nine months, you've got a problem! Acknowledge it and get on track to resolve the problem in you! Unless you gain control of your anger, you'll never progress in a spiritual manner with it. Keep ignoring the problem you have with anger and you'll never do anything appropriate with anger.

Too often, people deal with anger like a person who ignores or dismisses an illness. When they finally get to the doctor, he tells them they're nearly dead. Why wait so long? Sadly, many people wear their sickness like a badge of honor when they should go to the doctor and get healed instead. Likewise, there are some Christians who wear their anger like a badge of maturity. What a silly shame! Acknowledge it so you can deal with it.

So what is it about anger that as a problem?

Not acknowledging that it is a problem that must be overcome in your life.

To get a handle on your anger, you must first determine the extent to which you become angry. Analyze the previous times you became angry.

- What set you off?
- Did you behave properly or lose it?
- Was your response appropriate?

As you analyze your anger, you'll begin to see those areas in your life that remain un-surrendered to God and in rebellion. Prayerfully seek God to help you overcome the sin in those areas so you can respond properly in anger and not out of your carnal flesh nature.

Moses became angry and responded in an inappropriate manner. The result was God not permitting Moses to enter the Promised

Land. Imagine how Moses must have felt. After all the years wandering through the Wilderness, he could only look into the land from afar.

Angry behavior outside of God's design and plan bring consequences. For Moses, he couldn't enter the Promised Land. What about you? Have you ever reacted inappropriately in anger and then had to pay the consequence? This is one way God teaches His children to hear Him before they respond.

Moses' problem with anger didn't begin when he struck the rock instead of speaking to it as God had commanded. In fact, Moses problem with anger can be traced back to his days in Egypt when he murdered an Egyptian who was mistreating a Hebrew slave.

> *Now it came about in those days, when Moses had grown up, that he went out to his brethren and looked on their hard labors; and he saw an Egyptian beating a Hebrew, one of his brethren. So he looked this way and that, and when he saw there was no one around, he struck down the Egyptian and hid him in the sand.*
>
> *(Exodus 2:11-12)*

Moses' anger caused him to be a murderer. Notice that he "looked this way and that, and...saw there was no one around..." Like Moses, if you don't learn to control your anger when nobody is looking, you'll do terrible things.

Moses thought he was alone and that no one else was around except the Egyptian, so he killed him. Remember this important lesson, hidden things will be revealed. What you do in private will be discovered sooner or later. Your actions will betray you. Look at what happened to Moses:

> *And he went out the next day, and behold, two Hebrews were fighting with each other; and he said to the offender, "Why are you striking your companion?" But he said, "Who made you a prince or a judge over us? Are you intending to kill me, as you killed the Egyptian?" Then Moses was afraid, and said, "Surely the matter has become known."*
>
> (Exodus 2:13-14)

Moses fled into the wilderness where he remained for the next 40 years. Had he acknowledged the problem of his anger, the Egyptian probably would not have been killed. Nevertheless, God used this flaw in Moses' character to shape him into the man God would use to lead Israel out of bondage.

Deal With The Problem. You need to acknowledge the problem of your anger on previous occasions. You may have a lifestyle habit of anger that you're unaware of. You may have began getting angry and kicking your toys around when you were two years old and haven't stopped. Only now, you're kicking your family around or your tools or the dog. If you have to keep going back, month after month, year after year, apologizing for your behavior, it's time to admit you've got a problem with anger.

Acknowledge the problem with your anger and you can begin to deal with it. Hide it, and it will continue to simmer and stew and will eventually be discovered anyway. It's better to get a handle on it now rather than wait.

Let's go back to Moses. We've already read the Scripture in Numbers 20 where God told Moses to speak to the rock for water to come forth and Moses struck it with his rod instead. Why do you think Moses didn't heed God's instructions? Moses had grown weary of the unbelief and rebellion of the people. They didn't believe God and they didn't believe Moses—he'd had enough: "…Moses and Aaron gathered the assembly before the rock. And he said to them, "<u>Listen now, you rebels</u>; shall we bring forth water for you out of this rock?" (Num. 20:10).

Notice that Moses called the people "rebels." Moses was angry and his actions betrayed him. Once before, God told Moses to strike a rock so water could come out, but not this time.

Here is the lesson: Just because you're angry—even anger that God would permit—you don't have license to disobey God's instructions. You must remain faithful to what God has said and remain in control of your emotions.

If you are angry and do not follow God's principles, God interprets that as you're not believing Him. God sees that as a lack of trust and mistreatment of His holiness. Not following God's principles imposes your expression of the character of God upon Him, and that won't do!

This is much more than saying something inappropriate while you're angry. This has to do with what you think about your Heavenly Father and how He has told you to behave.

The psalmist said:

They angered him also at the waters of strife, so that it went ill with Moses

> *for their sakes: Because they provoked his spirit, so that he spake unadvisedly with his lips.*
>
> (Psalms 106:32-33 KJV)

Notice that because of Moses' anger with the people's rebellion, he spoke "unadvisedly with his lips." Moses spoke out of anger and his actions followed through.

Principle #2: Analyze the perspective of your adversary.

When you're angry, it's important to think through the other person's perspective. You have a perspective, as does the one who is agitating you. Therefore, you must think through the situation from their point of view. By analyzing their point of view, though their behavior or position may not be valid, it will help you to be more tolerant toward them and thus help keep you from sinning.

Moses missed this opportunity to remain in God's will. Instead of thinking about the problem of no water from the perspective of the people, he became intolerant of their complaining.

Had Moses taken the time to try and understand their point of view, he would have seen that these folk had been slaves all their lives in the land of Egypt where there was plenty of water and food. Yes. They were harshly treated in forced labor, but they had water.

Now, here they were in the middle of the wilderness, parched with thirst. There was no water in sight, just some man they barely trusted saying to speak to a rock to get water. Yeah! Right!

If Moses had looked at this situation from their perspective, not to validate the charge they made about wishing they had died in Egypt, but to understand it, his anger may have been less intense and his frustration not so great.

Moses' leadership had been questioned before. At the Red Sea, when Pharaoh and his army were after the Israelites, they complained out of fear that it would have been better for them to die in Egypt rather that in the wilderness.

Moses' own sister, Miriam, had attacked his leadership as had others in the congregation of the people. Though Miriam died at Kadesh in the wilderness (Num. 20:1), others took up her corrupt notion and continued to attack Moses. The people were thirsty and Moses didn't have any water.

This sets the stage for Moses' anger and abrupt action of striking the rock instead of speaking to it for water to come forth. Realize that there were thousands of people who needed to get water, not just one or two, and there was no digging equipment. They didn't know what they were going to do!

Have you ever been thirsty with no water in sight and no idea of where to get any? That is the situation Moses faced. Had he faced the problem from their perspective, he may have been a little more patient.

Moses should have known that the Israelites had little or no faith in God. Each time a problem surfaced, they would moan and complain. These folk had left Egypt like that; it was how they were. Moses should have decided to tolerate their unbelief and lead them into greater faith.

Moses had been leading the people according to God's plan and design, but it seemed like they were rarely near water. God was leading the people into areas where they would have to depend upon Him for all their sustenance, but they still weren't getting it. They looked at Moses and thought he was leading them to places with no water, causing all the voices of criticism to shout louder against Moses.

Likewise, if you are going to be God's leader, you'll have to learn that not everyone has the same level of faith you do. Once you take hold of that understanding, you can accept people where they are and lead them to where they should be.

Deliberately Work Through Your Anger

Had Moses understood that fact, he may have replaced his anger for compassion. Moses may have been able to better hear and obey the voice of God had he not judged the hearts of the people instead of their actions.

Anger can cloud your judgment and obscure the most obvious if you let it. That's why you must deliberately work through your anger.

If you have a problem with anger, acknowledge it so you can get on with your life. Look at the point of view of others so you can identify with them—not to excuse their behavior, but to understand their stance. Then, you will be able to lead them instead of miss the voice of God.

Remember, when everyone is attacking you, when all is arrayed against you, whether just or unjust, your response indicates your character. When it seems that nobody appreciates what you're doing or what's happening, your response shows who you are on the inside. That's why the apostles considered it a blessing to be counted worthy to suffer shame for the name of Jesus.

Do you consider it a blessing to be counted worthy to suffer shame for the name of Jesus? Will you pass the test?

Pray this prayer:

Heavenly Father. I'm a weak and frail human being. I sometimes harbor anger, bitterness, resentment, and jealousy, but now I want to be rid of it. I want to be counted worthy to suffer shame for the name of Jesus. I want godly character to come out of me every time I'm squeezed. Lord, do this in me is my prayer. Forgive me, Lord, for being an angry person. Thank you for showing me Your way. In Jesus' name. Amen.

Chapter Four

Violence—Anger's Deadly Ground

So it came about in the course of time that Cain brought an offering to the LORD of the fruit of the ground. And Abel, on his part also brought of the firstlings of his flock and of their fat portions. And the LORD had regard for Abel and for his offering; but for Cain and for his offering He had no regard. So Cain became very angry and his countenance fell. Then the LORD said to Cain, "Why are you angry? And why has your countenance fallen? "If you do well, will not your countenance be lifted up? And if you do not do well, sin is crouching at the door; and its desire is for you, but you must master it." And Cain told Abel his brother. And it came about when they were in the field, that Cain rose up against Abel his brother and killed him.

(Genesis 4:3-8)

VIOLENCE—ANGER'S DEADLY GROUND

"I don't know what happened. I...I just snapped and the next thing I knew, I hit her."

"We've discussed this before Mr. Roberts." said Minister Smith. "When you get angry, you lash out at the very ones who love you the most and hurt them. You must take control of your anger or you stand in danger of losing everything that is dear to you."

"What can I do? I feel like I'm at the end of my rope with nowhere else to turn."

Mr. Roberts' response to anger was unhealthy and unwise. First, by lashing out at those near him, he caused physical and emotional pain. He unjustly inflicted on others the pain and anguish roiling inside of him. Second, by using physical force, he slid down the slippery slope of violence that leads only to death. When Peter drew his sword to prevent Jesus' arrest, Jesus told him: "Put your sword back into its place; for all those who take up the sword shall perish by the sword" (Matt. 26:52). Third, by choosing violence, Mr. Roberts also chose to alienate his family, friends and co-workers. Violent men are lonely men.

The Danger of Violent Anger

The first mention of anger and violence in the Bible is found in the story of Cain and Abel, Adam and Eve's first sons (Gen. 4). Cain became angry with his brother Abel because God accepted Abel's offering and rejected his.

The word used to describe Cain's anger is "wroth" (Gen. 4:5). "But unto Cain and to his offering He had not respect, and Cain was very wroth." This word suggests a boiling, burning, hateful, revengeful anger.

Cain murdered his brother Abel while seething with anger toward him. While it may seem unbelievable that a man would murder his brother, it happens every day. Have you read the newspaper recently or listened to the nightly news? Have you talked to your neighbors recently?

Violence regularly sucks the lifeblood from those whom you love. You may know someone personally who has grieved in the grip of violence. Government officials seem to be utilizing all of the resources they have at their disposal but the problem of violence is not getting any better. Security personnel seem to be utilizing all of the factors and forces at their disposal as well, but the problem persists.

Regardless of where you live, violence has affected your life. Everyone has been victimized in some way; nobody is immune. But where does violence come from? And what is the world heading toward?

Destructive Responses To Anger Cause Pain And Suffering

I have been as angry as Cain was. However, just because I've been that angry doesn't mean I had no choice in how to respond.

Instead, I was faced with how to respond in light of the anger that if left unchecked could result in murder. The question of how to respond is one that must always be asked and appropriately answered.

Cain chose to respond destructively—first he argued with Abel and then he murdered him. When you are angry and respond destructively, not only do you destroy something, but you increase the intensity of the conflict as well.

The choice is yours. Now that you're angry, how will you respond? Will you respond destructively or will you respond constructively? Destructive responses destroy, while constructive responses decrease the conflict and minimize the intensity of the hostility that exists.

Cain could have responded constructively. God spoke to him before the murder and asked him to confront his anger. Notice what was lying at the door if Cain chose not to do well:

> *And the LORD said unto Cain, Why art thou wroth? and why is thy countenance fallen? If thou doest well, shalt thou not be accepted? and if thou doest not well, <u>sin lieth at the door</u>...*
> *(Gen. 4:6-7 KJV)*

Sin crouches at the door, waiting to seize the opportunity of our destructive responses. Like vultures waiting for a turn to tear into a dead body, sin seeks the opportunity to bring destruction and mayhem.

Cain could have done well, but he decided not to. Nevertheless, he was still responsible to master the situation that existed. He had to answer the question of how to respond when he was angry.

Why Are You Angry?

If you know that you're angry, do you know why?

We live in a world full of angry people. Little children get off the school bus angry. Why? He is angry when he got off the bus because he was angry when he got on the bus. Why did he get on the bus angry? Because he left home angry. Why did he leave home angry? Because he got out of bed angry. Why did he get out of bed angry? Because he went to sleep angry. Why did he go to sleep angry? Because he spent all day the day before angry.

Our entire society is angry. Everywhere we turn, somebody is angry.

Are you angry? Do you know why? Are

you angry because of something that has happened?

Cain should have questioned why he was angry. Was it because of what had been done?

Cain and his brother, Abel, each offered a sacrifice to God. Cain was angry because Abel's sacrifice was accepted and his was rejected. Therefore, the question was really not a matter of what's been done, but who did it

Jealous Anger Hurts The Defenseless

Many times we claim to be angry because of what has been done but we are really angry because of who did it. Husbands become angry with their wives for doing things they tolerate all day long from other women. Wives become angry with their husband about things they tolerate from others men. Children become angry with their parents for things they overlook from other folks all the time. Therefore, are we angry at what's been done, or simply angry because of who did it?

What about Cain? Is he angry because of who did something? Then whom should he be angry with? Should Cain be angry with

Abel for making an acceptable sacrifice, or God for rejecting his unacceptable sacrifice?

If Cain is angry with God, then why? Cain should be angry with himself; he's the one that offered the insufficient sacrifice. Likewise, if Cain is angry with Abel, then why? Abel has only done what is right in the eyes of God.

In reality, Cain was angry with himself. Often when people are angry with themselves, they take it out on whoever is most defenseless.

A child will be angry with his parents because they will not let him have any ice cream. On his way out of the kitchen, he'll hit his innocent brother who is sitting on the floor in the living room. The thought never crossed his mind to go back and kick his daddy for not letting him have the ice cream. He knew he wouldn't get away with that.

This is the mentality displayed in Cain. Sadly, it's prevalent throughout society; we pick on those who we think cannot defend themselves. The most victimized people in society are vulnerable because they're defenseless.

Your Response To Anger Is A Choice You Make

Rarely do we hear of a policeman being robbed. However, thugs will rob folks of their food stamps and just watch an armored truck go by with thousands, maybe millions of dollars inside. The truck is safe, because the guards have guns strapped to their hips. That's why criminals will bypass trucks carrying thousands of dollars and rob a cab driver of his only two fares of the day. Why? The cab driver is defenseless.

Your behavior is a choice. Even when you are angry, behavior is a choice. There is no acceptable excuse for violent behavior. Anger, especially, is not an acceptable excuse for violent behavior. No matter how angry you are you are responsible for your behavior. Your behavior is the result of a decision that you have made.

Society must get to the place where it holds people accountable for their behavior. Anger is no justification for violent, aggressive behavior. Parents need to step up to the plate and begin holding their children accountable.

Today, it seems that parents let their children get away with anything because they are angry. This must stop! Parents must begin training and conditioning their children to respond appropriately to their anger. Parents sometimes produce extremely violent children and then unleash them on the world and other children.

Learn To Respond To Anger In A Wholesome Manner

How did you respond the last time you were angry? What happened after your response? Was the situation better or was it worse? If the situation was worse, then there was a different way you could have responded.

Do you know why you were angry the last time? Were you angry at what had happened or because of who did it?

Begin now to train yourself to respond more wholesomely in your anger. Teach and train your children to respond more wholesomely as well. Remember, before Cain assaulted his brother, he argued with him, so stop arguing so much in your home.

> *For this is the message which you have heard from the beginning, that we should love one another; not as Cain, who was of the evil one, and slew his brother. And for what reason did he*

slay him? Because his deeds were evil, and his brother's were righteous.

(1 John 3:11-12)

Cain's problem was his sin. He was filled with violence instead of love. Cain did not love his brother because he was wicked. He became angry and assaulted his brother out of the violence that filled him. He wasn't right with God so he couldn't respond correctly to his anger.

Violence Comes From Being At Odds With God

Violence comes because you are at odds with God. Therefore, the only solution is to get your heart right with God. When God forgives you of sin, your anger can subside and your frustration can minimize itself. Then, you can accept folks for who they are.

As we think about Cain and Abel, we must realize that the sin didn't start with them; it started with momma and daddy. When Adam and Eve decided to disobey God, they set in motion a process that ultimately resulted in one of their boys killing the other one.

Gang Mentality Contributes To Gang Behavior

Another result of being at odds with God is the friends and associates you choose to hang with. The writer of Proverbs understood this when he gave his sons this counsel:

> My son, if sinners entice you,
> Do not consent.
> If they say, "Come with us,
> Let us lie in wait for blood,
> Let us ambush the innocent without cause;
> Let us swallow them alive like Sheol,
> Even whole, as those who go down to the pit;
> We shall find all kinds of precious wealth,
> We shall fill our houses with spoil;
> Throw in your lot with us,
> We shall all have one purse,"
> My son, do not walk in the way with them.
> Keep your feet from their path,
> For their feet run to evil,
> And they hasten to shed blood.
> Indeed, it is useless to spread the net
> In the eyes of any bird;
> But they lie in wait for their own blood;

> *They ambush their own lives.*
> *So are the ways of everyone who*
>   *gains by violence;*
> *It takes away the life of its possessors.*
>   (Prov. 1:10-19)

Notice that this same principle is expressed in Ephesians 5:11, "have no fellowship with the unfruitful deeds of darkness." We should not participate, support or engage in that which is wrong. Paul further wrote, "Lay hands suddenly on no man, neither be partaker of other men's sins: keep thyself pure" (1 Tim. 5:22 KJV).

Today, law enforcement warns of gang behavior in our local public schools. The clothing, colors, and conversation of many students support their findings. School personnel, when asked about events that happen during the course of the day, support the notion of active gang participation, even in the junior high schools.

Debate rages about the cause and the effects of gang activity on our youth and our society. What some say is the cause others say is just the effect. Others declare that gang activity arises because of the absence of adequate adult role models. The argument is also made that destructive gang activity increases because of the deterioration of the family support structure and network.

Attitudes That Foster Gang Behavior

While it is true that the absence of wholesome role models and the deterioration of the family exist, this does not validate destructive behavior. Destructive gang activity surfaces from a common source—gang mentality. Role models and family concerns contribute to a gang mentality, but it is the gang mentality that leads to gang behavior.

Attitude #1: I reject you because you accept my enemies.

This attitude plagues both children and adults. It is a mentality that says if you become a friend to my enemies, I have to part company with you. You become my enemy because you are a friend of my enemy, and whoever is favorable toward my enemies, regardless of whom it is, I become their enemy also. This is exactly what happens in gang activity.

Have you ever wondered how two folks can start to fight and before it's over there are 75 people involved? Have you ever wondered what causes people to hate folks they've never seen or met? It's because of the perception that they are friends of the enemy; therefore, they are enemies as well.

A gang mentality was present in the hearts of those who persecuted Jesus Christ.

We can see this illustrated in the gospel of Luke:

> *And it came to pass, when the time was come that he should be received up, he stedfastly set his face to go to Jerusalem, And sent messengers before his face: and they went, and entered into a village of the Samaritans, to make ready for him. And they did not receive him, because his face was as though he would go to Jerusalem.*
> (Luke 9:51-53 KJV)

Jesus was on His way to Jerusalem and was passing through Samaria to get there. Jesus sent some of his disciples to go into the city to prepare for his arrival, but the residents refused to receive Him. Why would they reject the coming of Jesus? Why were they upset at His presence?

The citizens of Samaria did not receive Jesus because His face was set toward Jerusalem.

Jews and Samaritans were bitter enemies during Jesus' day. The Jews hated the Samaritans and would not allow them to worship at the Temple. Likewise, the Samaritans hated the Jews because of their arrogance in who could and could not worship in Jerusalem (John 4:20-21).

Jesus was on His way to Jerusalem to celebrate with the Jews in the temple in Jerusalem. Therefore, the Samaritans refused to allow Jesus to spend the night. He was rejected because He was a friend of the Samaritan's enemy. This is what gives rise to gang mentality.

Attitude #2: *I accept you because you are an enemy to my enemies.*
Gangs have different colors. Robert is a member of a gang whose color is blue, while Michael is a member of a gang whose color is red. Reds are always at odds with blues, so when Robert sees a person talking to someone in Michael's gang, the red gang, then that person automatically becomes an enemy to Robert. Likewise, gang mentality accepts a person because they become an enemy to the gang enemy.

It was this kind of gang mentality and gang behavior that crucified Jesus. Look at the different groups of people that were involved in the crucifixion of Jesus:

- Judas and the multitude—Luke 22:47, "And while he yet spake, behold a multitude and he that was called Judas, <u>one of the twelve</u>, went before them and drew near unto Jesus to kiss Him."

- High Priest—Luke 22:54, "Then took Him and led Him and brought Him into the high priest's house."
- Soldiers—Luke 22:63, "And the men that held Jesus mocked Him and smote Him."
- Elders, Chief Priest, Scribes, Sanhedrin Council—Luke 22:66, "And as soon as it was day, the elders of the people and the chief priest and the scribes came together and led Him unto their council."
- Pilate—Luke 23:1, "And the whole multitude of them arose and led Him unto Pilate."
- King Herod—Luke 23:7, "And as soon as he knew that he belonged unto Herod's jurisdiction, he sent him to Herod, who himself also was at Jerusalem at that time."

Notice how the religious joined with the political to bring about Jesus' crucifixion. What do the chief priests, Pilate and King Herod have in common? Very little except a common enemy.

The idea of, "I accept you just because you are an enemy to my enemies" is the mentality that contributes to gang behavior. If you are an enemy to my enemies, you can't do any wrong; but if you are a friend to my enemies, you can't do any right.

It's a terrible tragedy that our children participate in gangs, made even more tragic when we realize that mommy and daddy have participated in gangs since before the child was born. Children learn gang behavior by observing the gang mentality of their parents. They have listened as their mother and father discussed issues and have seen that daddy is against something just because momma is for it. Or mother is against it just because daddy is for it.

Let me make it clearer. Children have heard their mother and father talk and argue about daddy not seeing any right in momma's relatives, and momma not seeing any right in daddy's relatives. Meanwhile daddy can't see any wrong on his side of the family and Mother can't see any wrong on her side of the family. That is the gang mentality.

Children know there are times that daddy ought to have stood up and said, "Momma, you are wrong!" Not his wife, to his mother! The children know that daddy should have said, "Grandmama, you're wrong!" But he wouldn't. This is gang mentality. Therefore, the child grows up thinking that relationship is thicker and stronger than right and wrong. They've learned this from their parents.

Sadly, children come to church and see gang mentality in their parents in regards to that as well. You may wonder how gang mentality surfaces in the church, but it's a "me VS them" thought process. For example, how often do children hear their parents make remarks about the church across the way? "Us VS them." Do you refuse to sit in a certain place because Sister So and So sits there? "Me VS them." It's gang mentality, and gang mentality leads to gang behavior.

Four Destructive Gang Mentalities To Avoid

You must learn to avoid destructive gang mentality and refuse to engage in destructive gang behavior. In order to do that, you must avoid destructive gang mentality. Here are the four things that will help you overcome this dangerous and debilitating condition.

Mentality #1: Accept principle above persons and personality.

You have probably observed a person that agreed with a principle until they found out it was their enemy who suggested it. Likewise, you've probably seen people stand against something until they discovered it was their friend who suggested it. These are examples of not placing principle above persons and personalities.

Mentality #2: Reject invalid principles regardless of the persons and the personalities involved.
You must not accept an invalid principle just because your friend suggested it. That is destructive gang mentality, which results in destructive gang behavior. Look at what happens: two students, members of opposing gangs, begin to fight. Though the one in my gang started the fight, I rush to help. It doesn't matter whether he's right or wrong. Why? He's in my gang.

That is the crux of the problem. People aren't looking at principles. If we're going to avoid this, we must elevate principle above persons and personalities.

Mentality #3: Never penalize people just because they are friends of your enemies.
Not everything about your enemies is bad. Just because your friend socializes with your enemy doesn't mean that your friend is agreeing with the wrong that is in your enemy.

Talking to a drunkard doesn't endorse alcohol. Likewise, if you see someone talking to a liar, that doesn't mean that lying is endorsed. Just because someone talks to your enemy doesn't mean they are endorsing the fact that you are enemies. Never penalize your friends just because they become friends to your enemies.

Some people have the capacity to do things that you don't have the capacity to do. There are folks who have the capacity to forgive others that you have not developed the capacity to forgive. For example: a daughter visits her father who is her mother's ex-husband, and mother becomes visibly upset. Why? If you are a friend to my enemy (my ex-husband) you also become my enemy. You must work hard at not penalizing a person just because they have the capacity to forgive that you don't have.

Parents sometimes parents mistreat their children. One child has the capacity to forgive while the other children choose not to forgive. Often, the children who do not forgive become at odds with the child who does.

Gang mentality produces gang behavior. Don't penalize folks because they can forgive others and you don't have the capacity to forgive them.

Mentality #4: Don't reward folks just because they won't forgive people.
Too often, we reward people who stay on our side, even if it means they must not forgive others. This gang mentality harbors hatred and freezes people in a lock-step of despair and unforgiveness.

Not forgiving others is nothing to be proud of. Instead, it is something to be cast far away from you. Jesus said:

For if you forgive men for their transgressions, your heavenly Father will also forgive you. But if you do not forgive men, then your Father will not forgive your transgressions.
(Matt. 6:14-15)

Violence And Gang Behavior

We've seen how gang behavior lead to the persecution and eventual crucifixion of Jesus. Today, we see the same thing played out in our schools, on our streets and highways, and around the world. When people come together sharing a common gang mentality, violence and destruction usually accompany them.

Too often we see on the headline news how a gang mentality leads to a feeding frenzy of anger-induced violence. Sadly, the most defenseless of society are usually the ones who pay the highest price.

Steer clear of any mentality that will pit you against "them." Remember the words of Jesus, "if you do not forgive men, then your Father will not forgive [you]" (Matt. 6:15).

Pray this prayer:

Heavenly Father. I repent for harboring any gang mentality or gang behavior in my life. Forgive me, Lord, for not taking the high road of forgiveness and choosing the low road of vengeance. Help me, Lord, to always be the first to forgive and the last to condemn. Help me see what You see in others that aren't like me. In Jesus' name. Amen.

CHAPTER FIVE

GODLY ANGER GETS RESULTS

And when they were come to the place, which is called Calvary, there they crucified him, and the malefactors, one on the right hand, and the other on the left. Then said Jesus, Father, forgive them; for they know not what they do.

(Luke 23:33-34 KJV)

Godly Anger Gets Results

"I'm angry about what happened, Mike. I'm not angry at Joe."

"Man. I'd be ready to kill him for what he did. You don't deserve to be treated like that."

"Mike! Surely you don't mean that. Joe is my friend. I can't condemn him for something that happened. Do you think that you know what was going through his mind? I know that I don't. But I do know this: Joe is my friend and I'm going to forgive him."

God gave us all of our emotions. Throughout this book, we've been discussing how to properly handle and respond to anger. Our responsibility is to learn how to use all of our emotions, including anger, to glorify God and breathe life into the situations in which we find ourselves.

Children are often taught to stifle their anger instead of how to express it in a constructive manner. Stifled anger is a raging volcano that seethes just below the surface, waiting to explode in a weak moment. By not learning wholesome ways to deal with anger, children often resort to violent outbursts that harm themselves and others.

Jesus was unafraid to express His anger. He didn't mince any words when talking with the Pharisees and Scribes about their religious hypocrisy, and He drove the wicked merchants out of the Temple with a whip—not once, but twice!

Jesus' anger was godly anger expressed in a godly manner. His anger was not fueled by jealousy, pride, self-promotion, or national zeal. It was motivated by the righteous indignation of one who knew God's heart. This is God's ideal for each one of us: to know His heart and express ourselves based upon that knowledge.

Godly anger gets results because God is

directing your behavior. Godly anger leads to godly responses, not violent outbursts or silent seething. Let's look at the life of Jesus at the time of His crucifixion to see ungodly anger in action.

Crucify Him! Crucify Him!

Imagine hearing a mob yelling to have you crucified after being arrested and tried by a kangaroo court. How would you feel, knowing that you were going to be executed based on trumped up charges and the lies of dishonest people?

Jesus faced that kind of situation. He was arrested and tried illegally by dishonest men seeking to protect their own religious and political interests. Jesus wasn't a player in the political games of 1st century Palestine, at least not deliberately. However, His very presence cast a threatening shadow over the ruling elite that caused them to strike out in anger, jealousy, greed and malice.

Then the whole body of them got up and brought Him before Pilate. And they began to accuse Him, saying, "We found this man misleading our nation and forbidding to pay taxes to Caesar, and saying that He Himself is Christ, a King." So Pilate asked Him, say-

ing, "Are You the King of the Jews?" And He answered him and said, "It is as you say." Then Pilate said to the chief priests and the crowds, "I find no guilt in this man." But they kept on insisting, saying, "He stirs up the people, teaching all over Judea, starting from Galilee even as far as this place."

When Pilate heard it, he asked whether the man was a Galilean. And when he learned that He belonged to Herod's jurisdiction, he sent Him to Herod, who himself also was in Jerusalem at that time.

> Now Herod was very glad when he saw Jesus; for he had wanted to see Him for a long time, because he had been hearing about Him and was hoping to see some sign performed by Him. And he questioned Him at some length; but He answered him nothing. And the chief priests and the scribes were standing there, accusing Him vehemently. And Herod with his soldiers, after treating Him with contempt and mocking Him, dressed Him in a gorgeous robe and sent Him back to Pilate. Now Herod and Pilate became friends with one another that very day; for before they had been enemies with each other.
>
> (Luke 23:1-12)

Notice how the religious, political and royal factions of society came together to accuse and defame Jesus. Notice as well, how Pilate and King Herod became friends and allies that day when before they had been enemies. Notice how a common enemy, Jesus, brought three angry groups together, each seeking to carryout their own particular agenda and forward their own particular cause.

However, also notice Jesus' response to all that was set before Him. From the time He was arrested till the crucifixion was finished, Jesus could have called the hosts of heaven to come and rescue Him. Had He let the anger of others control Him instead of Him exercising control, that may well have happened. Nevertheless, Jesus remained composed and did not allow the forces arrayed against Him to prevail.

The forces that came against Jesus to crucify Him expended tremendous energy to no avail. Yes. Jesus was crucified. Yes. Jesus died on the cross. However, Jesus arose victorious from the tomb and conquered both death and the grave! The very thing Jesus' enemies wanted to accomplish was thwarted through the mighty power of God in Jesus.

Invest Your Energy

Jesus knew that to successfully complete His mission on earth, He could not be deterred from His purpose. Jesus chose to invest His energy in what was productive and constructive, rather than spend His energy fruitlessly.

You must work through your anger in the same way. You must invest your energy in a manner that revitalizes the relationship. You must remain solution oriented instead of being steered into a fruitless blind alley of despair. Like Jesus, you don't have time to focus on how awful you're hurting, focus instead on a solution.

For example, if you are injured in an automobile accident and are experiencing blood loss, the emergency room personnel aren't going to agonize over how bloody their clothes are getting, they're going to work to stop the flow of blood! There is no time to worry about how to get that stain out! You're bleeding! They are focused and solution oriented.

Too often, people spend more time complaining about the problem than looking for a way to solve it. If you have a flat tire, you have a choice. You can take the spare out of the trunk and put it on the car, or stand there and gripe about the flat. Which one do you suppose will get you going faster? Invest your energy don't squander it.

Learn How To Deal With Your Adversaries

We saw in Luke 23 how Pilate respected Herod's jurisdiction. Pilate was the Roman official in charge of Palestine, while Herod was over Galilee. Scripture says that Herod had desired to see Jesus for some time, and Pilate made that possible. Pilate allowed Herod to fulfill a long-awaited desire.

Everybody wants something—personal recognition, personal gratification or recognition for a job well done. One sure way to deal with your adversary is to give him what he wants. By doing so, you've lessened the intensity of the contention between you and opened door of reconciliation.

Pilate lost nothing by sending Jesus to Herod and instead gained an important ally. By sending Jesus to Herod, Pilate gave the king an opportunity to make an important decision of government. However, since Herod found nothing to condemn Jesus for, he sent Jesus back to Pilate.

This is an important principle for you to learn. People often become aggravated because somebody infringed upon their territory. People are very protective of what they consider to be their responsibility, so when someone else horns in, they often become angry.

Too many infringements will bring such animosity that the two become enemies and wind up competing with each other in other things as well. Sadly, the two who are competing against each other are often members of the same team and should be working together instead of against each other.

Often, the only way to bridge the gap is to relinquish what we consider to be "ours" to the other person. By doing so, like Pilate and Herod, friendship may result and the relationship saved.

Forgive Your Enemies

Another way to revitalize a relationship that has gone sour is to be the first to forgive. Sometimes the only answer is absolute forgiveness, which takes you out of the penalty phase. Stop trying to "get even" with the other person and instead get right with them.

God wants us to get to the place where we can look a person in the eye who has mistreated us and say, "I forgive you" and mean it. Too often, we wait until the other person is willing to forgive or ask for forgiveness before we're willing to forgive. Well, what if they're never ready? Does that mean we will never forgive them?

Jesus didn't wait until the people who crucified Him asked for forgiveness. While on the cross, He looked at the people and said, "Father, forgive them for they know not what they do" (Luke 23:34). Jesus was trying to revitalize His relationship with His enemies. He knew they would behave differently if they knew what they were doing, so He was able to forgive them in advance.

Paul wrote, "But God demonstrates His own love toward us, in that while we were yet sinners, Christ died for us" (Romans 5:8). Before we ever asked God to forgive us, Christ died for us. Likewise, we should demonstrate love for others by forgiving them before they ask.

Peter stood on the Day of Pentecost and preached to the multitude saying, "...let all the house of Israel know for certain that God has made Him both Lord and Christ—this Jesus whom you crucified" (Acts 2:36). Some of those present when Peter preached were also present when Jesus was crucified. Because of Jesus' act of forgiveness, these people were pricked in their hearts and sought the Lord.

Often, people will behave a certain way out of ignorance. These men and women had acted out of ignorance toward Jesus but now they had the facts. Now they could see what Jesus was all about and they immediately repented and turned to God.

Forgive So You Can Be Forgiven

A principle that runs throughout Scripture is that of sowing and reaping. A farmer plants corn in order to harvest corn. He cannot plant corn and expect to harvest wheat.

This principle is true in life as well. Scripture teaches that God desires mercy over sacrifice (Hosea 6:6 KJV). Therefore, as you sow mercy, you'll reap mercy. "For judgment is without mercy to the one who has shown no mercy. Mercy triumphs over judgment" (James 2:13 NKJV).

Jesus said to forgive others so your Father in Heaven can forgive you: "For if you forgive others for their transgressions, your heavenly Father will also forgive you. But if you do not forgive others, then your Father will not forgive your transgressions" (Matt. 6:14-15).

Therefore, in light of God's Word, how can we hold a grudge against somebody and feel justified in doing so? What gives us the right to act as judge, jury, prosecuting attorney and victim in the kangaroo court of our mind? Who do we think we are? God?

This attitude divides churches, families, friends and co-workers. It's time to bury the hatchet...and not in someone's back!

Are you holding a grudge against someone? If so, it's time to drop the charges and forgive them. Furthermore, it's time for you to repent and ask God to forgive you for harboring a root of bitterness against this person.

Next, you must do what you can to rectify the situation with the other party. Whether you go visit them and ask forgiveness, call them on the telephone, or write, whatever you must do, make an effort to reconcile. Don't wait until after the person is dead and there's nothing you can do. Make amends now, not later.

Do you want God to forgive you? Then forgive others—it's that simple!

Anger is no reason to harbor unforgiveness. Work through your anger. Identify the problem and deal with it. Don't let anger steer you, you steer the anger. Turn it into something of value instead of wasted energy and a sour stomach.

Look Beyond The Person To The Source

It's time we learned to look past the situation to discern the source of the problem. What motivates sin? Who is the master practitioner of sin? Who moves people to do ungodly acts?

Satan!

If you're going to be angry, focus your anger on the root of the problem, not the vessel. If you discovered that a burglar had taken money and possessions from your home while you were out, you'd feel violated. It's natural to feel that way. This would be followed by the emotion of anger usually directed toward the person who stole from you. But who motivated the person to steal?

When you realize it's the devil that has stolen from you, you can still love the person and focus your anger where it should be focused. Furthermore, you may become motivated to work against the kingdom of darkness by leading people out of it and into the Kingdom of Jesus Christ.

Adam and Eve ate of the tree of life and thus ushered sin into God's creation. Along with sin came sickness and death, conditions that still plague fallen humanity. Should we blame Eve for taking the fruit and offering it to Adam? Through her, should we also look at other women as the cause of pain and suffering in our world today? Absolutely not! This would be a travesty and the greatest injustice. Look instead to the one who deceived Eve—Satan. That old serpent was the first to betray God and beckoned others to follow.

Get angry with Satan! Godly anger gets results when God directed.

When you visit a sick friend in the hospital, do you get angry with them or with the doctors? No. You have compassion on them and pray that the doctors will be able to help them. Direct your anger toward the enemy, not the victims of the enemy.

Godly Anger Gets Results

When God directs your anger, you'll find that reconciliation, restoration and renewal come with it. Godly anger gets results because self is moved out of the way so God can move. When you allow Satan to direct your anger the result is jealousy, destruction, division and death.

You can choose today what you're going to do the next time anger flares. Will you choose life or will you choose death? Will you choose to bless or to curse? Look at these Scriptures:

> ...choose for yourselves this day whom you will serve...But as for me and my house, we will serve the LORD.
> (Josh. 24:15 NKJV)

> Behold, I set before you today a blessing and a curse: the blessing, if you obey the commandments of the LORD your God which I command you today; and the curse, if you do not obey the commandments of the LORD your God, but turn aside from the way which I command you today...
> (Deut. 11:26-28 NKJV)

> See, I have set before you today life and good, death and evil, in that I command you today to love the LORD your God, to walk in His ways, and to keep His commandments, His statutes, and His judgments, that you may live and multiply; and the LORD your God will bless you...
> (Deut. 30:15-16 NKJV)

Make your choice. With God, you can be both good and angry. Pray this prayer:

Heavenly Father. You have set before me choices that I must make. Therefore, I surrender all my anger to You to use as You see fit. Help me through Your Holy Spirit to make godly choices and to speak life and not death—restoration and not devastation.

Thank You, Lord, for helping me fulfill Your Great Commission to go into the world and make disciples. Make me a witness of You, Lord, so that people will see You and not me.

Finally, Lord. Remove from me all of my own agendas. Help me to live like Jesus when He said, "Not my will, Father, but thy will be done." In Jesus' mighty name I pray. Amen.

About the Author

John Marshall has given more than 2,000 presentations throughout the United States, helping thousands of people with his practical and penetrating teaching style. He is an author, editor, media producer, facilitator for conflict resolution, motivational speaker, preacher, public relations director, teacher, trainer, and relationship consultant. He received his bachelor's degree from Freed-Hardeman University, master's degree in counseling from Theological University of America, and has done additional graduate work at University of Memphis and Southern Christian University. He is a staff writer

JOHN MARSHALL

for *The Christian Echo* and *The Revivalist* magazine, a member of the Alumni Advisory Board of Freed-Hardeman University, and preaches for Graceview Church of Christ in Stone Mountain, Georgia, where he and his family live.

OTHER BOOKS BY JOHN MARSHALL

Final Answer:
You Asked, God Answered

God Knows!
There Is No Need to Worry

God, Listen!
Prayers That God Always Answers
(includes addiction-recovery guide)

My God !
Who He Is Will Change Your Life

The Power of the Tongue
What You Say Is What You Get

Success Is a God Idea

Show Me the Money
7 Exercises That Build Economic Strength

Contact Information

For further information about John Marshall, his ministry, and other ministry resources, please contact him at

Mail:
John Marshall
P. O. Box 878
Pine Lake Georgia 30072

Web:
www.graceview.us

Email:
jdm@graceview.us

Phone:
(404) 297-9050
(404) 316-5525

www.ingramcontent.com/pod-product-compliance
Lightning Source LLC
Chambersburg PA
CBHW031257290426
44109CB00012B/620